CHANT
Your
GOALS

By

Ron Piscitelli

CHANT
Your
GOALS

By Ron Piscitelli

This book is a work of non fiction. Names and places have been changed to protect the privacy of all individuals. The events and situations are true.

The author of this book does not dispense medical advice or prescribe the use of any technique as a form of treatment for physical or medical problems without the advice of a physician, either directly or indirectly. The intent of the author is only to offer information of a general nature to help you in your quest for emotional and spiritual well-being. In the event you use any of the information in this book for yourself, which is your constitutional right, the author and the publisher assume no responsibility for your actions. specifically disclaim any liability that is incurred form the use of the application of the contents of this product. This product is designed to provide competent and reliable information regarding the subject matter covered. However, it is sold with the understanding that the author and publisher are not engaged in rendering legal, financial, or other professional advice. Laws and practices often vary form state to state and if legal or other expert assistance is required, the services of a professional should be sought. The author and publisher

First Edition

ISBN 13: 978-1475245745

ISBN 10: 1475245742

Chant Your Goals

Table of Contents

Chapters   **Page**

Ron Piscitelli
Chant Your Goals

Introduction

Many years ago, I listened to self improvement tapes recorded by Earl Nightingale. One of the statements he made was; "Whatever the mind can conceive and believe, it can achieve."

This statement is the basis of everything this book is about.

The two most important aspects in achieving your goals are conceiving your desires (things you love), and understanding how to change your self image (building belief).

Let's start by thinking about the words in that statement.

Conceive – The dictionary defines conceive as: *a* **:** to take into one's mind. *b* **:** to form a conception of **:** imagine **:** to apprehend by reason or imagination

What can you think about? Can you conceive making a million dollars a year, a billion dollars a year or inventing something? How about conceiving a big house or going on great vacations?

Believe – When we hear the word believe, it seems simple. The question is much deeper than if someone tells us something and we believe them. The real issue is how to change our self image to believe it is happening in our lives now.

It doesn't matter if the idea is right or wrong, if our mind believes it, and our self image believes it, it happens in our lives.

An example is the old world belief that the world was flat. No one could change people's opinion about the subject because their belief was so strong. As a result, ships would not venture out too far from land going west from Europe.

If you can change a belief, you can create the life you want. The majority of this book is to give you ways to change your beliefs and self image. This is a subject you have to take seriously. If it were easy to change, everyone would be doing it. It is easy when using the right methods. That is what this book is all about.

It will be up to you to go out in the world and find the things you love. Desire is the starting point. As you start making your list of items you love and situations you would love to experience in your life, your list will expand.

I could have made this book one thousand pages long by filling it with advice for every situation in life. I could have also filled these pages with trivial advice as so many inspirational books on the market today do. When you get off the main message of how to create your dreams, you dilute the important information. This book is kept "right to the point."

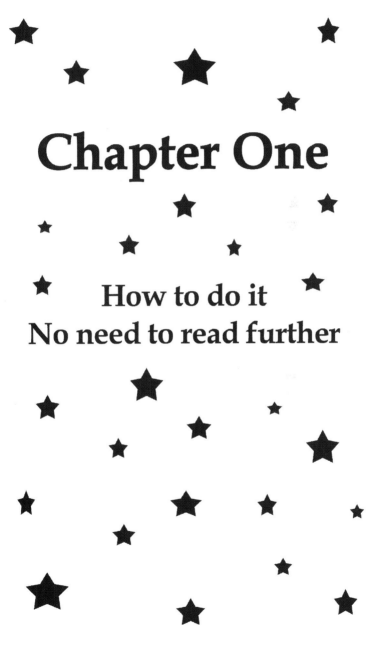

Chapter One

How to do it
No need to read further

Read No Further

There is no need to read any chapter other than this first chapter. All you will need to know to get anything you want and to change your self image will come in this short first chapter.

Gravity

Do you need to know all the reasons gravity happens?
Do you need to know all the scientific equations?
All you need to know is if you jump out of a second story building, you will fall to the ground. If you drop a glass, it will break. Once you know the basics, you follow the rules.

It is the same with getting what you want out of life. Once you know how, then all the reasons why are of little consequence. If you really want to know more of the why, read the rest of this book. I will explain the why in simple terms.

Okay, so how do you get what you want out of life?

The basic way how;

Focus on what you want!

1. Start by listing everything you want, including material things and non material things.

2. List as many things as you can. Your list can be short or long. There are no limitations. You can have it all.

3. Be sure your list is full of things you love.

4. It is okay to change your mind if you find you love something else more.

5. Write a statement for each of the items you want. The statement should read: "I love (whatever it is you want)." If you want a new Ferrari, you would say, "I love a new red Ferrari." The more details the better.

6. Say your statement out loud when you go to bed at night.

7. Say your statement out loud when you get up in the morning.

8. Chant your statement all day long as much as you can. Stay focused on what you want.

9. Do all you can do each day in what you are presently doing. Be the best you can be. Improve things.

10. If you get a negative thought, say "cancel, cancel" and replace it with one of your statements.

11. Be grateful. Appreciate all the good you now have.

12. If you are depressed or down, it means you are not focused on your goals coming true.
You are focusing on your goals not coming true.
Immediately think of all the things you are thankful for; then chant your goals and get back to feeling good.

13. Being happy, being excited and feeling good confirms that you are moving towards your goals. You are in a state of believing they are coming true.

14. Relax and have faith in the system.

So there you have it. It is that simple. Start enjoying life.

If it is that simple, why are people not getting what they want?

The "System" of focus works whether you believe in it or not. If you talk to people about things, you can tell what is happening in their lives by their conversation. Have you ever heard people say any of the following statements?

1. The economy is bad.
2. I can't afford that.
3. If I eat that piece of chocolate I will gain ten pounds.
4. I cannot find a job.
5. I am tired, I am lonely, I have no money, etc…

I could go on and on. I am sure you have heard others express thousands of negative statements.

Whether they believe it or not, they are focusing on the negative things in life. Each time they think the thought, it is affirming the negative thing they want to avoid. In turn, that statement becomes their reality.

So start right now performing these steps. Do not wait to finish this book. Each day you wait is another day that passes.

Ron Piscitelli
Chant Your Goals

★ **Chapter Two**

How the
Universe/God Works

The System

How does the "System" work? First let's talk about who we are. We are a piece of the "Whole" which includes life and everything we see in life. We are connected to the "Whole." From here on, I am going to refer to life and everything in it as the "System."

Whatever it is that the "System" is, we are part of it. We are the co-creators. We think of something and it becomes a reality. A good analogy is something that I heard about the war in Iraq. An expert in the armed forces said that in Iraq if you were going to blow up a target, a person on the ground would focus a laser towards a building and the jet overhead would fire a missile and destroy the building.

Life works the same way in the "System." We focus on the end result of something we want. That is what our job is to do. Then, the job of the "System" is to make it happen, manifest it. By making it happen, it could be to lead us to the right people, or inspirations of what to do. It provides us with the energy to take action. We do not have to force it. **It pulls us.** If we are forcing it, we are going against our present self image.

Most people are in the habit of looking at what resources they currently have and then they limit what they can have or what they can do. They live within their means and shut down their desires. They think, "I now have just a little money so what can I buy with it?" What they should do is look for what they want, something they love no matter the cost, and think of the end result of their having and using it. Then they should allow the "System" to make it happen.

Let me say it again: "The way to get what you want in life is to first seek out things you love and then focus on them as if you have them." The "System" will make it happen in your life.

Needs

Needs are a natural way the "System" works. You have heard of the saying, "Necessity is the mother of invention." It's true, because unless there is a need, the "System" cannot work. The "System" of creating things cannot get jump started. If you have a need, you let go of the problem and perhaps instantly or after a day or two, ideas and inspirations come to mind. Most of us have experienced this process.

If you can imagine way back when nothing was invented, we went to the lake to drink water. We got down on all fours and drank like other animals did. It was difficult to drink this way. Perhaps it was a problem and a solution was needed. Then, someone got the idea to cup his hand and bring the water up to his mouth. From that someone broke a coconut in half and used it for water. When you really think of it, the way we drink liquids today is not that far off from that coconut. Yes glasses come in different shapes, colors and some are made of different materials, but they basically are the same idea, except someone had the need to have a better looking container. This is a simple reference as to how the mind creates from needs. The great news is that this "System" can also be used to bring to us things we love or circumstances that we love.

Wants

It is easy to see when there is a need, how the mind works. When you focus on the things you love, you are using the "System" to produce beyond needs. You now are producing wants. You are focusing on the end result of what you want and the mind gives you inspirations, ideas, attracts the right people, ideal situations and ultimately gives you unlimited energy to create your desires.

The more you focus on the thing you desire, the more your self image becomes that thing and manifests it into your life. It is that simple, yet, if I ask people to name me three items they would love to have, they hesitate with an answer. They think and think. How can the "System" bring you your wants, if you are in the habit of suppressing them or not taking the time to identify them?

At this point, write down at least three things that you love and want. If you have to think about it and cannot come up with three things right away, you will have your answer as to why you are not getting ahead.

Ron Piscitelli
Chant Your Goals

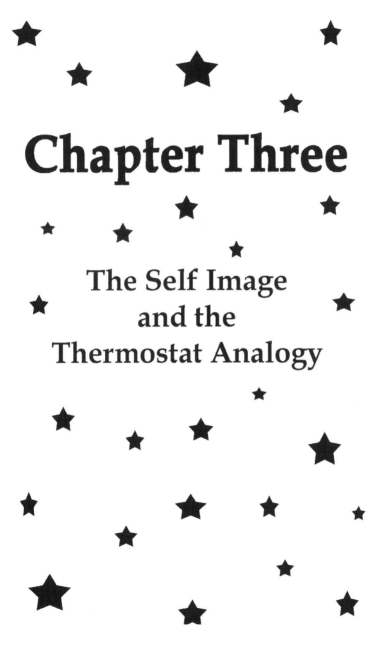

Chapter Three

The Self Image
and the
Thermostat Analogy

The Self Image

The self image is a place in your mind where there is a picture of every belief you have. If you are talking about money, it is the amount of money you make on a yearly basis and the assets you have. If you want to know what a person's self image is, look at what they now have. There is no reason to judge a person. The point is to know what a person's self image is on a given subject. The good news is that there are ways to change the self image.

Remember that the mind is like a computer. The difference between what comes out of computers is the software. People work in the same way. We are all equal in that we all have the same mind as computers have the same hardware. The difference in results on the outside is the self image, which is like the software. It is the pictures (beliefs) each person holds on each subject that gives different results.

There are many pictures (beliefs) a person holds, such as vocation, money/income, assets, family, love, physical-health, spiritual needs and friendships, plus a million other sub categories.

The self image works like a temperature gauge. Let's say you set a thermostat to 70 degrees. If the room temperature drops below 68 degrees, the heater turns on automatically to bring the temperature back up to 70 degrees. If the temperature goes up past 72 degrees, the air conditioner turns on and brings the temperature back to 70 degrees. That zone between 68 and 72 degrees is called the comfort zone. If you want to change the temperature in the room, you would simply go to the thermostat and change it to the temperature you desire. The heater or air conditioner will automatically bring the temperature into the comfort zone.

Your beliefs, the pictures you hold, work in the same way as a thermostat. If you are now making $50,000 a year and you want to increase your yearly income to $100,000, your best results will come first by changing your self image. Perhaps this has happened to you. You want to make more money, so you work harder. You end up making more money that month and then your car breaks down, or you lose a different account. Your income always seems to even out over the course of a couple of months.

To make permanent changes in your income, start with changing your self image. Just as one changes the setting to change the temperature, you need to change the picture (belief) in your mind to that of the one you want to accomplish.

Chapter Four

How habits
are formed

Brain cells and dendrites

When we are born, we have a brain filled with cells and these cells are connected with each other by connectors called dendrites. Another way to look at this is like cities in the USA. Think of the USA before the Pilgrims landed with woods and wilderness. Then cities sprung up over time, Boston, New York, Chicago and Detroit. This is just an example and not the order of cities in America.

These cities were connected with roads. Eventually these roads grew to super highways. The mind of a child works in the same manner. Those brain cells are like cities. Each thought the child has creates a pathway between brain cells. A thought that is repeated becomes a habit. A habit creates a pathway. A belief creates a pathway.

The longer the same thought is held repeatedly, it creates a deeper pathway between the brain cells. Then, a stronger habit is formed, like those super highways between cities.

It would be ridiculous to think you could drive from Boston to New York in a straight line through people's back yards. It is much easier to follow route 95 to New York. That is how the mind works as we get older. Let's use making money as an example. We think of things in the same way as we have over the years. That is why it is so hard to change your self image for example, more money. Every thought you have just follows that path of non money. You have to change to a making more money consciousness.

Now let's think of how our thoughts are formed. We hear something and a pathway between the brain cells is created. This starts from the time we are born.

Our first day of life to our eleventh year, 70% of our beliefs and habits are formed. Even if the beliefs are wrong, they take root. If a child hears around the house "we have no money, money is tight," …et cetera, those thoughts are creating a pathway in the mind of that child for habitual "lack" when it comes to money.

These non-effective habits keep us in a state of non money and run our lives in every area of performance. It brings up the question; "If these habits or deep pathways between the brain cells are formed, is there any hope to change?" The answer is yes! We need to know how. Not knowing how is the reason so few ever change their reality from what it is today.

Next we will get into the "how" of making changes.

Chapter Five

Auto suggestion
Affirmations

After I graduated college, my plan of action was to change my circumstances. When I read <u>Think and</u> <u>Grow Rich</u>, I was struck by the term Napoleon Hill used at the beginning of his chapter on autosuggestion. He stated, "Autosuggestion, the ***medium*** for influencing the subconscious mind." Why didn't he just say, "The <u>**way**</u> to influence the subconscious mind." So I went to my dictionary to find the definition of medium. "From the Latin, middle. Something, as an intermediate course of action that occupies a position or has a condition midway between extremes." My first thought was, "What on earth does that mean? Extremes?" That is when I started to realize that to change my self image was much more complicated then originally thought.

Then I started to think of where I had heard the word medium used in the past. I heard of it used in a séance. That is where a person supposedly contacts another world.

So am I to believe that to change my self image I needed to reach another world? Perhaps another world is an extreme concept, but I realized that I would have to do something other than think I could just change my self image by using my will power.

Years later I thought of something that happened to me by accident. I was coaching someone for their business and was encouraging them to use autosuggestion. At the time I thought autosuggestion meant to say a statement as if it already happened. That is what I read in many books as to the way to change your self image. In those types of books, an example would be as follows. Let's say you want to affirm a new red Ferrari. Their technique was; "I now own a red Ferrari," affirmed in the present tense.

I was asserting just that, but whenever I stated it, a little voice inside of me would say, "but I love a Porsche."

I didn't give it much thought at the time. About two months later, I got the Porsche. I then realized that when I said a statement to myself like, "I now own a red Ferrari," a little voice inside of me would speak up and say, "no you don't." That little voice actually cancelled out the affirmation. In my case, I didn't love the Ferrari so my voice confirmed what was true, "I loved the Porsche." The actual affirmation was about the Porsche.

I realized that when a person makes an affirmation, for example, "I am now a millionaire," a little voice inside of him has an opinion. If he is not presently a millionaire, it would say, "No you are not!" That little voice is meant to guard his self image.

While it does protect him, it also works against him if he wants to change.

As you are reading this book, if you notice, your little voice either accepts what I say, questions it or contemplates it. The point is, if you listen closely, you can recognize that the little voice is there.

Then I had chills running down my spine. Perhaps changing is really simple. All I would have to do is write out my affirmations in a way that the little voice inside would agree with me instead of doubting me. I tried doing it on other affirmations. I tried it on my weight and body. I simply wrote statements declaring what I loved. "I love a 34 inch waist." While I did not have a 34 inch waist at the time, my little voice could not argue with me about it, because I did love a 34 inch waist. I will go into the use of "Love" in chapter nine.

I started losing weight while drinking a case of Coke a week. I am not advocating drinking Coke.

I am saying the outer world is a reflection of the inner. To change, I must reach the inner world with properly worded affirmations that work.

There are many programs out there on changing your self image that recognize the little doubting inner voice. One of them uses a music CD that has subliminal messages inside. The reason they are subliminal is to bypass that inner voice. Another program is the Silva Mind Method. In that program, a person would bypass that inner doubting voice by going down into alpha, which is basically slowing a person's brainwaves and going almost into a meditative state.
The alpha state is like when you wake up in the morning, where you are aware, yet your eyes are closed. In this state, when you do your affirmations or visualize your goals, your doubting inner voice is sleeping.

Both of these programs are effective, but constantly chanting your goals using love is the most effective way. Changing your self image is a 24 hours, 7 days per week job.

I interviewed many successful people. I asked what made them successful. I listened to their conversations of how they achieved their goals and their self talk. Their words were a constant belief and affirmation of what they thought possible, reflecting what they loved. I asked one person in particular who owned a huge company. He said he loved what he did. That statement is an affirmation. His little voice could not argue with him because it was true.

He did love what he was doing. I asked how he grew his business to having over 20,000 accounts. He always kept thinking of how he could get 20,000 accounts.

He now thinks about how he can get 100,000 accounts. I have no doubt that he will get them. His focus is on what he wants.

Webster's dictionary defines <u>affirmation</u> as, "To declare or maintain to be true. Affirmation comes from Latin, affirmare: ad-, to + firmare, to strengthen."
The dictionary defines <u>autosuggestion</u> as, "The process by which a person promotes self acceptance of an opinion, belief, or plan of action."

To change the self image, all you have to do is state what you want in a manner that keeps your inner voice from disagreeing with you.

The reason you say it over and over is because you need to change that pathway we talked about in the last chapter on habits.

When habitual thought changes, it then influences the self image and you are the result of your self image. Once the self image is changed, you will attract people, opportunities, resources and the energy to accomplish your goal without effort. You will be going with the flow of life and not fighting it.

When you use the word love in your affirmation, not only do you agree with your inner voice, you are also adding the emotional element to your statement. It is important to add emotions to your affirmations. After chanting your affirmation with the word love in it, your affirmation will become very familiar. That is because you will have created a new pathway between brain cells.

A natural result will be that you will attract similar thoughts using the phrase "I now" as if you already posses the item or circumstance you are seeking.

Talk about being excited. I decided I could have anything in the world that I could want. I wrote this book so I could pass this information on to my kids. I hope you keep it simple and just spend each day searching for things and conditions that you love.

Chapter Six

Visualization
and the
Flick back/flick up

Another way to change the self image is through visualization. The dictionary defines visualization as: "To form a mental image or vision of." To change your self image through visualization, you would picture in your mind the situation you would like in your life as if it is already happening. You would see the situation through your eyes as if you were living it now. Many people visualize seeing the situation as if they are watching TV. The best technique is to be in the situation.

An example of how <u>not</u> to do it would be if you were watching the I Love Lucy show. Do you remember watching the show? You are watching it from the sidelines. You laugh at the jokes and almost go into a hypnotic state. You can see the whole apartment as a spectator. This is how most people visualize. This is <u>not</u> the best way.

Now, to make the visualization work best, imagine sitting in Lucy's living room. See it as if you are sitting there. Watch Lucy come from the kitchen, and see Ricky come in the door and greet you. You ask Ricky a question. Then you look around the apartment from the standpoint of being in the room. Perhaps you ask Lucy where the rest room is and you go there. Look at yourself in their mirror. You comb your hair. Visualize in as much detail as possible. Use all five senses.

If an example of one of your goals is a new car, go out and drive as many cars as you can until you find the one you love. Not the one you can afford. Once you find that car, see all of the features, noticing as many details as possible. Next, visualize yourself in the car. Note the dashboard. Engage the sensory pleasure of touching the steering wheel. Inhale the new car smell.

Listen to the horn. Turn on the radio and enjoy it playing your favorite music. Drive in your driveway and get out of the car. Do with the new car as you do now with your present car. This is what you should do with each one of your goals.

While chanting affirmations, it is most effective to bring emotions into the statement. That is why we use the word love. When visualizing, you also want to bring successful emotions into it. A great technique is called the "flick back, flick up" technique. I first heard this from Lou Tice from the Pacific Institute in Seattle. While visualizing, go back in time to when you had a victory, when you accomplished something and were successful. It could even be a compliment you received from someone you highly respected. Relive that moment. Sense the feelings you experienced that were of a successful nature.

You had excitement. Let those feelings well up inside of you and bring those feelings to your present visualization.

You are borrowing sentiments of success and using them for your goals. This flicking back to a prior success, and then flicking up to your present visualization, associates successful feelings for your future goals.

People use this technique all the time now, but it is by chance. They do not know they are doing it. They just do it naturally. That is what confidence is all about. You did something. You made a cake. Everyone loved the taste as you did, and now, every time you make a cake, you know you can do it.

The problem arises when you have had a negative experience. The bad feelings are so strong that you lose confidence in ever trying it again.

Let's say you decided to sell magazines as a kid. If you were lucky, all of your relatives bought some, but if one of them criticized you and did not buy, this could have been humiliating.

You may never want to feel that feeling again. The very thought of sales prompts pictures and emotions of failure in your mind.

This is where the deliberate use of visualizations, borrowing feelings from past successes and using them for a new affirmation can work in your favor to build confidence in anything you want to do. The mind does not know the difference between an actual event or one imagined. So a visualization done over and over can move you towards that which you want in your life.

When doing affirmations or auto suggestions, as stated in the last chapter, I suggested to fool the mind by stating them in the manner of loving whatever it is that you want. You want to silence that inner voice from giving negative thoughts to your goals.

With visualizations, you view them as if they are already accomplished. You view them in the now as if you already possess the goal. Sprinkle in successful emotions from when you had a victory in the past and voila, you have the most effective way to change your self image!

Ron Piscitelli
Chant Your Goals

Chapter Seven

How do you know
if you are on
the right track

Emotions

If you want to know if you are on the right track, all you have to do is think of how you feel. Feel great, and you are heading towards your goal. Feel down, and you believe that you cannot achieve your goal. These emotions work on each area of your life. You could be excited and happy about a relationship. That means you believe you have one and at the same time could be down about your financial situation.

Emotions are like an indicator gauge in your car. If your gas gauge needle is pointing to "E" it means you need to put in gas. If it is pointing to "F" it means you have plenty of gas. At the same time, you have many other gauges in your car. You have a temperature gauge and a speedometer. One gauge indicates all is fine while another could mean things are not fine.

For example, you could have plenty of gas while your temperature gauge could indicate a serious problem if too high.

When thinking of an area of your life, see how you feel on the subject. If you are feeling great, put that aside for a moment. Work on the one that has you feeling down. This is when it is time to set a goal for something you love. Then construct an affirmation. Visualize it in a way that is effective in creating that situation in your life, as stated in the last two chapters. Your emotions are your indicator gauge as to where you are in relation to the goals you have.

Many years back, I read in a book that a person should keep track of his moods so that he can be very effective in sales. It stated that a person has peak moments every month and should only visit prospective clients when he is at a peak. He should avoid prospects when in a down mood.

So I started listing my moods every day and kept track. On the days that I felt down, I did office work. On the days I felt great, I would go out to market. At the end of the month I noticed that I was always feeling down. Perhaps it was my excuse to avoid marketing. Then one day when I was down, a call came in and I got a new very profitable client. I was very excited and I started jumping up and down with my wife as we held hands. That is when I realized that I was in control of my emotions. If it were really a cycle, even the great new client wouldn't have changed my mood.

Instead of looking for reasons for being down, you can create affirmations and visualizations that can get you excited. You can fool the mind. Do this continually and you will find that it becomes a habit. You can create habits in your brain that fill you with confidence.

Most people, including people we view as successful, do not know this. I am sure you know people who are successful in business, then have an out of shape body. You know people who have wonderful loving relationships, and have financial issues. If people really knew how they were successful in one area of their lives, they would know how to be so in other areas. You now know how to make changes in each area of your life and you now know if you are on the right track with your emotions.

There is one other thing to be aware of with emotions. The reason it seems so natural to have negative expectations and negative emotions is because of the way we were conditioned from the time we were born. Imagine when a baby is born. He really has no way to communicate.

If that baby is hungry or has a wet diaper, the only way he can tell the mother is by crying. Crying is a negative. What is the reward for crying? The mother comes and comforts the baby. The mother hugs and gives the baby love, then changes the diaper or feeds the baby. The baby is given a reward of the best thing life has to offer, _**love**_. This is mental conditioning as Pavlov learned with his dogs and bell. Pavlov took a group of dogs and rang a bell. Then he fed them a steak. After this procedure was repeated many times, all he had to do was ring the bell and the dogs would salivate as if they would be fed steak, even though no steak was in sight.

Mental conditioning is another name for a deep rooted habit.

Now this baby grows up to be an adult. When there is the slightest struggle, adults get negative. On a subconscious level, the pathways of habit play out with negatives.

The only difference is that a person is not rewarded with love. Usually we call this negative person a bad word or we try to avoid them. If this person is trying to reach a goal and gets negative, instead of love as a reward, it brings into this person's life the opposite of what he wants. Then the habit repeated over and over creates such a deep groove of a non effective way to reach the goal that it will take a great effort to change. The great news again is that you can change. That is why it is important to seek goals that you love. Love makes all the difference. <u>If you love it, it will be easy to think about over and over in your mind.</u>

PS If you see someone acting negatively, you now know that they are in need of a hug.

Ron Piscitelli
Chant Your Goals

Chapter Eight

Love is all you need

All you need is love.

We have heard this many times in our lives. Christ talked about love. Love thy neighbor as thyself. Even the Beatles told us, "All you need is love."

The dictionary has many definitions. Most talk about affection towards another. There was another definition that I did find interesting. "An intense emotional attachment (attraction) for a treasured object." I found it interesting because I was taught to not desire material things. One of the reasons so few actually use the self image to produce wants is this guilt with which we are raised.

Love is so important in the world, yet it is something suppressed in us as children. We are taught not to want the things we love. In my case, my mother was wonderful.

She gave me love and that was the best thing for which I am grateful. On the other hand, I was always talked out of the things I wanted. I realize that kids ask for everything, all the time. What parent could provide it? Perhaps it is also about money. The problem with this is that it ends up becoming a habit of suppressing wants.

I am the author of children's books that encourage self employment called Kids Playing Business. In one of the books, I talked about a child who wanted a large purple ball when she went shopping with her mother. The mother told the child that she could have the ball she wanted, but she would have to earn the money. The mother taught the child to find ways to earn the money and purchase the ball on her own. This is the way it should be. Instead of parents saying no, they should encourage the child to find things they love, then help them find ways to earn the money.

I have asked many people if they had an Aladdin's Lamp and a magic Genie who would grant them unlimited wishes, what they would want. Most do not have an answer. Then I asked them to keep it simple and tell me one thing, remembering that they still had unlimited wishes so not to think that this limits their choices. Most people still could not answer. Try this yourself. How can your self image be formed to attract things to you, if you do not know what you want? Obviously, this is not something people are taught to do.

In chapter two of this book I said the following statement and it is worth repeating.

"It is easy to see when there is a need, how the mind works. When you focus on the things you love, you are using the "System" to produce beyond needs. You now are producing wants. You are focusing on the end result of what you want and the mind gives you inspirations, ideas, attracts the right people, ideal situations and ultimately gives you unlimited energy to create your desires.

The more you focus on the thing you desire; your self image becomes that thing and manifests it into your life. It is that simple, yet, if I ask people to name me three items they would love to have, they hesitate with an answer. They think and think. How can the 'System' bring you your wants if you are in the habit of suppressing them or not taking the time to identify them?"

When I use the word desire it is the same thing as saying you love something. So start listing things you love. It is okay if you do not know what you want. You have to start looking for things out there. I am not saying you should use your rent money to buy a diamond ring. Just find the diamond you love, and visualize it on your finger. Let the "System" do the rest.

I am not saying to worship material things. Material things are nothing more than something a person created. If you see yourself as a quality person, why not enjoy the quality creations of other quality people? You are not better than someone else because you have better material things. Please keep material things in perspective. A great thought regarding material things is in relationship to your affirmations on income.

If you desire to make one million dollars a year, do you know what a million dollars is? If you are now making $50,000 a year, you can relate to what that amount of money will buy, but can you relate to a million dollars a year? To make a million dollars, it will be easier if you have affirmations about material things that will require making that amount per year. Then your mind can relate.

I was coaching a young man who told me he wanted to make a billion dollars. I asked him about the material things that he desired in his life. He told me he would like to get married some day. He would like to own a home with a fence around it. He wanted a nice car and would like to take a couple vacations per year. I asked him why he would need a billion dollars when his goals would need only about $100,000 per year?

He had no answer. I am not saying don't go for the billion. I am saying that your mind has to relate to a billion dollars by the needs and goals you have. I told him to find things he loved that would take a billion dollars, or start first by making that $100,000 a year and go from there. Now if he told me that he wanted to own the San Diego Chargers, then he would require a billion dollars.

Go out today and start finding things you love. Here are a couple ideas.

What kind of house do you love? Go look at some open houses.

What kind of car do you love? Go test drive some.

What kind of clothes do you love?

What kind of savings do you love?

What do you love to do for a business?

What kind of body do you love?

What kind of friends would you love to have?

What kind of a relationship would you love to have?

Do this exercise for any type thing you want to attract in your life. The more you write things down, the more ideas will come to you. Remember, these things have to be what you love. It is easy to write things down because others have them, or to write down things just because they cost a lot of money, or to write down things to impress a friend. I did that when I said "I now own a red Ferrari." I am thankful I wrote it because it taught me to use love as the way to affirm what I want. I didn't love the Ferrari. I loved the Porsche and I still do now that I have one.

If you plan to be self employed or if you plan to work for someone, do what you love. If you have a hobby or an interest, this could be a great idea for a business.

When I first read about doing a business that you love, I thought I was different, because I loved my family and I loved America with the free enterprise system. What business could I ever get in loving my family? In my spare time I was painting pictures with my family as the theme. Then I realized I could write kid's books about America with the topic of self employment and my family as characters. I wrote them because I loved doing it. I did not need motivation to work on my books. It came naturally from within. Making money at it was just a side benefit.

I heard Rush Limbaugh telling about how he struggled with income until his late forties. His advice was; "Find what you love to do and remain dedicated to it."

Many years back I had just lost a big account that produced about $8,000 a month in income. So an adjustment was needed in my lifestyle.

I was walking in downtown San Diego and I noticed this huge framed print of the Empire State Building in a store window. It was 6 feet tall and 4 feet wide. I fell in love with it.

At the time I did not know about loving objects to get them into my life. I couldn't believe I loved it so much. I told my wife about it. She said not to think about it because we could not afford it. At that moment she reminded me of my mother growing up. She was right regarding money in my bank account, but I loved the picture too much to stop thinking of it. I could not get it off of my mind. The only reason I didn't get it at that moment was I had no place to hang it. I am an artist in my spare time. I have my paintings on every wall of my house. I was going crazy in my mind. About two months later, I realized that I had a map of the county of San Diego next to my desk in my office which was the exact size of that painting.

I found a spot for the map in my shipping department and the minute the spot opened up next to my desk, I hurried to the store to buy the picture.

The point of this story is that when you love something, it is easy to keep thinking of it. If you have to force yourself to think of something, then it is not what you love. Many people do not take the time to go out and find things they love, or they suppress the desire. My advice is to find as many things to fall in love with as you possibly can. If you jot them down and realize that you love something better, remove the item and add the new one. Never stop doing this. Then chant that you love it, (I will get into chanting in a later chapter) and visualize using it in your life.

Ron Piscitelli
Chant Your Goals

Chapter Nine

Love and Hate

Love and Hate

Another thing I discovered was the use of chanting the words love and hate. I was working out one day and my trainer, Matt, told me to eat more broccoli. I said I hated broccoli. He said, "Why do you have to say you hate it? You are using too much emotion when it comes to food." I decided to just say I loved broccoli. As a result, I actually started to desire it. Then I decided to say that I hated things that I wanted to get rid of in my life. I smoked pot since college for about 30 years. I tried to quit it many times. Never could. Then I smoked all I wanted, but every time I did I said, "I hate smoking pot." All of a sudden one day I didn't have the need to smoke. It was not as if I made a big deal about giving it up or made a big announcement. It was as if I had never done it. It has been over six years and still no desire for it. No big deal.

Then I tried using the love/hate method with spaghetti. I wrote an Italian cookbook from my mother's recipes. It was my connection to my mother who had since died. My impression of spaghetti at the time was that it made me fat. I stopped having the desire for it, because of my mantra, "I hate spaghetti."

If you knew me, you would know my attachment to Chinese food. For example, I would take a trip to Boston for a week. I calculated that I would eat 21 meals while there, three meals a day for seven days, all Chinese. My mother-in-law invited us to dinner on Thanksgiving. I said that I would come, but I could eat turkey any time in San Diego. I was going to have Chinese food first then visit. You can imagine the stir this caused, (no pun intended), but I did not care. I was hooked on Boston area Chinese food. Then I chanted that I hated it while still eating it when I wanted. Guess what?

I no longer have the emotion of it and I never gave up a thing. I did give up the wording I used when I talked about it. Instead of always saying that I loved it, I said I hated it. Let's review. I said I loved the Porsche and I got one. I said I loved a 34 inch waist and I lost two sizes, while eating what I wanted and drinking a case of Coke a week. I said that I hated Chinese food, spaghetti and pot which resulted in my not being emotionally involved any longer.

Someone questioned me as to why fat people do not lose weight. They proclaimed all fat people hate being fat. I agreed that it was true. They do hate being fat. The reason they do not lose weight is because of the other things that they say. They also say they cannot stick to a diet. They say they love the wrong foods. They say they wish they could lose but can't. They say diets don't work, because once you are off of them you gain more weight back.

They also may say if I eat this cake, I will gain five pounds. These are just some of the negative statements people are conditioned to say. Can you see the non effective self talk?

I was talking to a person who loved chocolate. She believed that chocolate was the reason she was fat. I personally believe it is not the chocolate, but the affirmation she is placing on it. So I merely stated, "Why not give up chocolate by chanting that you hate it?" I explained that you will just end up losing the desire for it. She said that she would never say that because she loved it too much. She could not see how her words were creating pathways in her mind that formed her self image and produced her outer world. She was so deeply in the habit that the mere mentioning of saying she hated chocolate was too much out of her comfort zone to even understand the premise.

If you word your affirmations correctly with the use of the words love and hate, you could eat the chocolate and be thin.

If you chant you love broccoli, and chant you hate chocolate, you would love broccoli as much as you previously loved chocolate. It is the pathways between brain cells that become deep grooved habits and become the self image that dictates your outer world. You would be replacing chocolate with the new love of broccoli. You will never miss the chocolate if done in this manner. YOU ARE ACTING OUT OF YOUR SELF IMAGE. The solution is to change your self image to produce the results you are seeking.

At first, I was amazed at the resistance when I was trying to help someone break a habit as I did for the person with the chocolate. At least the person admitted she had a chocolate fixation.

I was talking with a person who could not quit smoking cigarettes. He hated smoking, but without realizing it, he was saying over and over that he could not quit. He tried many times over and over for the past 40 years. He is 65 years old today. He now sneaks outside his back door to smoke, because he doesn't want his family to know. I suggested he smoke all he wants, (he smokes all he wants now anyway only with guilt) and chant that he hates cigarettes whenever he thinks about them. Then not have any other thoughts about them.

He got upset with me as if I were insulting him. I did not ask him to suffer by using his will power. I did not ask him to quit cold turkey. I did not ask him to bring me the broomstick of the Wicked Witch of the West. All I said was to keep smoking all you want, and say that you hate them.

Can you see how strong the self image is and how it can run your life? Even doing something as easy as changing your wording can go against how you habitually think. I strongly recommend changing your wording by inserting love about the things and habits you would like to change for the better in your life. I also strongly recommend changing your wording by inserting hate about the things and habits you would like to remove from your life.

It works. Do it today!

Chapter Ten

Chant, Chant and Chant some more

What is chanting? When I refer to chanting, I am indicating taking one of your affirmations and repeating it, saying it over and over all day long as much as you can. I could have said repeat your statement all day long, but chanting emphasizes the importance I want to place on this practice.

Why chant? The real question is, "Why repeat your affirmations again and again?" The reason is because you want to change your thinking. A statement repeated becomes a habit and starts to take root in your mind. If you remember in chapter four, I talked about brain cells and how habits are formed. This is worth repeating here.

When we are born, we have a mind filled with brain cells and these cells are connected with each other by connectors called dendrites. Another way to look at this is like cities in the USA. Think of the USA before the Pilgrims landed with woods and wilderness. Then cities sprung up over time, Boston, New York, Chicago and Detroit. This is just an example and not the order of cities in America.

These cities were connected with roads. Eventually these roads grew to super highways. The mind of a child works in the same manner. Those brain cells are like cities. Each thought the child has creates a pathway between brain cells. A thought that is repeated becomes a habit. A habit creates a pathway. A belief creates a pathway. The longer the same thought is done over and over, it creates a deeper pathway between the brain cells. A stronger habit is formed. Almost like those super highways between cities.

When you hold a long time belief of something, such as making $50,000 a year, it is like that super highway between the brain cells in your mind. Every time you think about money, you automatically travel this pathway of earning $50,000 a year. Now to change that habitual thought or belief to one of making $100,000 a year, a new pathway must be created. It will take great effort to change. One of your new affirmations could be, "I love $100,000 in income every year." I say one of them, because you want to have many different ones all about the $100,000 per year. If you love what you do and say you own a restaurant, you would have another affirmation saying, "I love $10,000 per month of business at my restaurant."

It may take $20,000 per month after over-head costs, but this is what you must figure out with your business. When chanting your affirmation, your mind cannot understand $10,000 net. It only hears $10,000. If you want to make $10,000 a month, you have to take over-head costs into consideration and make the adjustment. If you are not doing what you love, you could start with just the $10,000 a month affirmation.

When I say it will take great effort, I am talking about the effort to chant your statement as much as you can every day. Those old pathways will be fighting you. It will be more comfortable to think the old thoughts. The more you chant the new affirmations, the easier it gets. You will then notice that these new thoughts will attract other similar thoughts.

Chant them enough and when you think of money, your thoughts will automatically go down this new pathway in your mind to make $100,000 per year. As this new pathway becomes a super highway, your self image will change and attract you to your goal.

Many people ask how long it will take to change the self image. One thing depends on how deep the former belief is. The deeper it is the more chanting and visualizing the new belief will be needed. Another aspect will be what your world looks like today. Let's say you talk with your brothers, sisters and parents. Let's say that they always repeat a statement that your family has bad luck with making money. This becomes a reinforcement of the former belief each time it is talked about. This happens especially when you tell others of your plans to change.

It may not come from your family. It could be reinforced from TV shows, radio stations, newspapers, friends or various other ways.

I had an experience once that made me realize how quickly an affirmation or new thought about a subject can change in your life. I watched someone being interviewed on TV about their business. I had my cleaning company at the time and I thought while driving in my car, how I would respond if a reporter asked me a question about my business. I didn't know about affirmations at the time. I was just fantasizing about someone interviewing me. After I got out of my car, I didn't think about it again. The next day, I received two calls from local TV stations. The NBC affiliate in San Diego called for my opinion on the illegal immigrant situation regarding the cleaning industry. I declined that interview, because that subject did not pertain to me.

The ABC affiliate also called and wanted to do a story on my company, because one of the anchor people used my service and loved the quality I provided. I couldn't get over it. I thought about it one day and the next day a reporter was at my office with a cameraman.

This incident taught me that an affirmation can happen instantly depending on your prior beliefs on the subject you are affirming. Another belief that holds us back is the belief that change takes time. That could be another mantra, "I love that goals happen instantly once an affirmation is chanted out loud." It is logical to say that if you want your goals to happen faster, then you should avoid negative people and spend all of your spare time chanting your new affirmations. In addition, visualize yourself in your desired goal as if it is happening now filled with winning emotions you borrowed from past successes.

I have a computer in my office at home. Years ago it was the only computer in my house. Many people used it such as my wife, kids, a house guest that stayed for a month plus a couple of office assistants I had helping me with my books. Today, each member of my family has her own. My computer is new, but some of the files go back to that original computer. When I first started writing this book, I named it "Chanting for Success." I wrote the first couple of chapters and then saved the file. When I went back to add another chapter, I noticed a file called "Chant" dating back to 2005. That was six years ago. I loved what it said about chanting and the benefits. I added it here in the next paragraph. I have no idea how it got on my computer. My kids do not remember making the file, nor do I. It could have been that house guest or one of my assistants. I never chanted and never had the slightest desire to do so. I know I never created it.

I wish I could credit the person who wrote it.

Here it is.

In many cultures and civilizations, chanting, a form of vocal meditation, has endured through the ages. Practiced by many people around the world seeking greater health, a sense of well-being, enlightenment, and a connection to the divine, **chanting unites the mind, body, emotions,** (*this is a great way to enhance your affirmation*) and breath through vocal sounding. This unification can open and nurture your creativity, lower stress levels, and teach you to become fully alert and in the moment.

Chanting lets you raise the level of your own vibration to a higher spiritual state. You can chant as an invocation **or to set intention.** *I especially like "to set intention."* Reciting even the simplest chant can bolster a flagging spirit, hone the mind, and produce natural painkillers within the brain.

While chanting, you may feel energy surging through your physical body or joy entering your heart. Chanting can liberate and ground you simultaneously because it allows your soul to soar freely while compelling you to focus on the here and now.

I love this description of chanting. I was using chanting because it worked with my affirmations. There are many statements in that paragraph that seem to verify why it works with affirmations. My thanks go out to the person who wrote it.

One last thought regarding chanting, don't let the word "Chant" lead your thoughts down the wrong path. I was talking to a person who was having weight-issues in his life. He had no success in getting thinner. I told him about my way of changing.

He said, "Chanting reminds me of the Hara Krishnas." He was a Christian. I said, "I am using it to change my thinking; it is not used in a religious way. Plus, I think the Christians chanted long before any other group did."

We ended our conversation with his saying that if I used a word like repeat instead of chant, he would try my method. If you want to change and you have not had success with any other method up until now, I hope you see the merits in this method without getting caught up with a word.

An example of chanting is something I heard said by Anthony Robbins in his CD program, <u>Get the Edge,</u> before he made his millions.

In the program he was talking about a time when he was running up and down the beach jogging while repeating this phrase day after day after day.

"Money circulates in my life in avalanches of abundance. All my dreams, goals and desires are met instantaneously, because I am one with God and God is everything."

Mr. Robbins never said he chanted. This was an affirmation he repeated over and over. Repeating something over and over is the same as chanting. No one can argue with his results regarding his goals which are very impressive.

Ron Piscitelli
Chant Your Goals

Ron Piscitelli
Chant Your Goals

Chapter Eleven

Act as if
and
Ask

Ask

Have you ever noticed that you have a voice inside of you that asks questions all the time? Have you ever asked yourself, "why did I do that?" How about, "why did I say that?" Another common one is, "why am I so stupid?" We all ask ourselves questions all day long. The problem is that the questions we are asking produce the wrong type of answers. The answer you would get from a question like, "why did I say that," is that you are always saying stupid things, or that you just made a fool out of yourself.

When you ask a self defeating question like the ones I just listed, you end up with a negative statement about yourself. When you repeat these statements, they become affirmations of what you do not want to happen in your life.

Asking questions is a good thing. We have heard the statement from the bible, "Ask and you shall receive." They are referring to asking great questions. Here are a few examples of effective questions to ask.

1. What can I do to make a million dollars a year in my business?

2. How can I solve this problem I am having?

3. How can I change my self image?

You can ask questions about anything you want to accomplish. Can you see how a positive answer will come from a properly worded question? It does not matter if you have a problem to solve, or if you seek knowledge as to how to achieve your goals.

By crafting a positive question, you can receive answers for any issue. The responses you receive from your questions, become your reality when you focus on their end result.

Don't be fooled thinking that questions from others are innocent of consequences. They reinforce all the reasons for which you may not be succeeding with your goals.
Recently, I went to a lecture given by one of the people from the movie, The Secret. I couldn't believe this person showed us a list of the reasons people fail and asked us to highlight ones that pertained to us. I started looking for the items that pertained to me. Then I thought, "why on earth would I want to contemplate why I have failed in the past?" If I did fail at anything, it was because I lost focus on my goal. This is the only reason anyone who has not achieved what they want out of life has failed.

The only reason I should attend a lecture is to hear encouragement to find things that I love, and then spend all of my time focusing on the end result of what I seek. It doesn't have to be any more difficult. I do not want to pick on the person from The Secret. The same idea was in the book, Think and Grow Rich. It demonstrates the 31 reasons that people fail. This same approach is in many books. I know these authors are trying to help people achieve their goals. They mean well, but many people in our lives mean well. If these people have skewed opinions about achieving goals, I cannot allow myself to be caught up in their beliefs.

The bottom line is to achieve your goals. If you ask questions the right way, it can be a tremendous tool that will bring you the answers you seek.

Act as if

Another way to approach changing your self image is to act "as if" it is already happening. As an example, you could go test drive new cars as if you were actually buying one. Once you find the one that you love, you can visualize it as if it is already yours. If you want to increase your business, you could visualize how it will look when you reach your goals.

My favorite way to act "as if" is by giving an imaginative lecture to a group of people at a meeting, in a class, at a college or on a talk show, explaining how I achieved my goal.

Let's say you plan to build a million dollar business. Then picture yourself giving a talk at a business meeting explaining how you did it.

Do not worry if you are not sure how you did it. Explain it the best way you can. You will be surprised how much fun this is. The more pretend talks you give, the more the content will expand. You will have more to say from many different angles. These statements become affirmations that stay with you.

My favorite place to lecture is in my car on the way to appointments. After repeating this many times, I feel "as if" I actually gave the presentation.

Ron Piscitelli
Chant Your Goals

Chapter Twelve

Gratitude
and
Faith

Gratitude

The whole purpose of every aspect of changing your thinking and self image is to keep your mind positive. There are many times when things around us affect our mental well being. Some books on the subject of changing your self image say that to get in a more positive and happy feeling, all you have to do is change your thoughts to your goals as if they are happening now. I concur. The problem for me was that when I was in a down mood, I found it difficult to get out of it. Was I the only person on earth who could not do this? It almost felt pleasurable to stay in the bad emotional mood.

Then one day I read about gratitude. I heard about it many times before. I would always say I was grateful and was thankful for all the good I had in my life. I did that when I was feeling good and positive.

So I tried it when I was in a down emotional mood for the first time. I was amazed! I immediately got out of those negative feelings and felt great.

When you are grateful and appreciate all the good you have in your life, you can change your mood to one of happiness. No matter the issue, there is always someone worse off. There is an old quote, "I felt sorry for myself because my legs hurt until I met a man with no legs." When you are thankful for the good in your life, it makes you feel great. This is the type of mental atmosphere you want to have at all times. Once in that good mood again, it will be easy to get back on track chanting your goals and visualizing them as if they are happening now.

Faith

Having faith is another aspect of keeping your mind positive. You need to have faith and believe in this "System" of changing your self image. If not, doubts creep into your mind. What are doubts? Doubts are negative affirmations. A negative affirmation will produce habits which then influence your self image. Everything in your life is a reflection of the self image. To change the outer self, you have to change the inner self first.

A person I am coaching has set a goal to have 100 clients for his service each paying $400 per month. This amount of business would bring in around $40,000 to his business every month. He is chanting this affirmation. He asked me a question the other day saying he was confused as to how to achieve his goal.

He said he wasn't sure of the size of his classes or the size of his office and I could see confusion in his eyes.

I thought about it for a moment, and then realized that this is what we all do when we set goals. We try to figure out how to achieve them. What we should do is find things we love. Chant them in a way as to bypass our little doubting voice inside. Then use the word love in our affirmation. Then focus our attention on the end result of the thing we love and let go. It is God's job or the Universe's job to manifest it in our lives. We do not have to think about the how. We just need to focus on the end result of the goal we seek.

In the case of the person I am coaching, when he thinks of the way to do it and has a problem as to the how, his well intentioned affirmation now becomes a negative one.

Worrying is a negative way to use his thinking. This negative thought will obviously create the opposite of what he wants in his life.

Do today's work.

He cannot do tomorrow's work today. He does not need to worry about how something will get done. All he needs to do is today's work in the best, most professional manner possible. If my coaching client just does today's work, and continues the chanting of his affirmations, the right way to do things will become apparent. Perhaps he will attract ten new clients right away. At that point he will know more about the landscape of his business than he now knows.

Regarding achieving your goals, the idea is to climb the first mountain on your journey. Once on top, the view of the next part of the journey will be clearer. This is where faith comes in. Just have faith in the system. If you do catch yourself feeling down, start being thankful for all that you do have going for you now. Another way to look at it is if you were to take a road trip from San Diego to Boston. There is no doubt if you follow the highway that points to the northeast and you follow the signs, you will eventually get there. How do you really know it will lead you there? Faith. It's your faith in the US highway system. If you ever took the trip as I have, it seemed as if it were going to take forever. It was the faith in the system that kept me going. This is the same type faith you need to have in goal achievement.

Keep it simple, have faith, be thankful and do all you can do today in the most professional manner. "Faith means believing in things when common sense tells you not to."
From the movie, Miracle on 34th Street.

Chapter Thirteen

This and That

This chapter deals with situations that affect your thinking. The first one is about the people with whom you associate. We have all heard this statement before; "You are judged by the friends that you keep." The question is, "why is this statement true?" Here is an example.

If you want to be thin, it would be better for you to associate with people in shape. I know when I am with people who are athletic; the conversation is more about fitness. One time I was telling my trainer that every Saturday I take my family to eat at our favorite Italian restaurant. He wanted me to attend some function at his gym instead. I said this was our favorite activity and I would not miss it. He was shocked at my statement. He said, "Activity? I consider an activity taking my family to throw a Frisbee or something athletic. When I think of eating, it is to satisfy my hunger. Your definition of an activity is going out to eat." I was dumbfounded for a moment.

I had to think about that. He was right. If I told over weight people about eating out as an activity, they would have agreed with me and reinforced my habit of non-effective weight loss thinking. Because of my association with my personal trainer, my habitual thoughts of eating and my body were changing.

I recounted this subject with a millionaire friend of mine who is successful in his business. I asked him if he knew of any millionaires I could interview for this book. He said he played cards with a bunch of them. He said, "All they talk about is money. They talk about investments, or talk about opportunities." I can see why they make money. It is what is on their minds. That is their focus.

Associations influence your thinking. For example, I sat with a few of my employees who were former Navy guys at a Starbucks. Every time a woman walked by, they would stare. I was trying to talk business, and they were constantly distracted. I kept turning around to see who they were looking at. Finally I told them to stop looking unless the woman walking by was a ten. These guys would look at anyone, even someone I would rate a one, with hunger in their eyes. I was tired of turning my head not to mention the fact that it would interrupt my thoughts of business. By these guys associating with me, we were focused on business. By me associating with them, our focus was on sex. If what you get out of life is based upon your focus, it is very important to place yourself in situations where you can keep the proper focus.

Think of every area of your life, such as business, vocation, health/fitness, relationships, spiritual and all the subcategories. If you want advice, seek out someone successful in that area.

If you want advice on building your business, ask someone successful. Most people talk to their friends or family. Unless those people are successful in business, what possible answer do you think you are going to get? Most likely something negative such as, "Most businesses fail in the first five years."

I was at a seminar one time when a fat person asked the speaker after the conclusion of the meeting, how to lose weight. The speaker was over-weight too. The lecturer told this person to eat raw almonds. She said eating raw almonds was the secret to losing weight. I started laughing. I asked myself, "Why would a fat person ask a fat person how to lose weight?"

This happens all the time in every area of life. My advice is to either find successful people in the area of life you would like to change, or find books by successful people in the area you would like to change.

Love they neighbor or enemy as thyself.

You have heard this statement many times. Why is this important? It is important in the pursuit of your goals. When you do to others as you would want them to do to you, it makes you feel good about yourself. If you are feeling good about yourself and you are focusing on your goals, it keeps you from thinking of some act you are not proud of. When you do something wrong, even if you think it was right, you end up thinking about the situation over and over trying to justify why you are right. This takes your focus away from your goals and deep down, is a negative thought.

For your own sake, the best way to do business or interact with other people is to realize you will have all the abundance you want if you build your self image in the proper manner. This whole book is about changing your self image. There is unlimited abundance in this world. You are not in competition with anyone. When you do business with others, make everyone win in the transaction. It feels good and frees your mind to think the right thoughts to help you attain your goals.

What if someone does us wrong, don't we have the right to be upset? That is a question we have all asked ourselves. Sometimes we all get caught up in revenge, but this is the worst thing on which to waste our thoughts. If someone does something wrong to us, the worst part of it is that it takes our thoughts away from our goals and where we want to go, to thinking about why that person did us wrong.

At one point in my janitorial company, one of my managers stole some of my accounts and started his own business. At first I was shocked, because I helped this person a great deal. Then I decided to forgive him. I realized that my income was a result of my self image and not that of another person. If I lost an account, I would replace it as long as my self image was of the income I wanted. If I wanted more income, I would have to work on my thinking. I hope you can see how this helps free your thinking so you can focus on the end result you seek with your goals.

The next time someone does you wrong, remember that the real wrong is the perpetual negative thoughts you will hold forever, rolling around in your mind, going over it adinfinitum. You are losing precious time that you could be spending focusing on the end results of the goals you desire.

Chapter Fourteen

Final Thoughts

There was a statement in the Bible (Matthew 17:20) that says, "…If ye have faith as a grain of mustard seed, ye shall say unto this mountain, remove hence to yonder place; and it shall remove; and nothing shall be impossible unto you."

If you have faith in this method, which is part of the "System" as small as a mustard seed, you will achieve your goals.

If you have not had success with any other method talked about in any other self help or goal achieving book, try this method. I was shocked at my positive results. They came so easily. By just trying my method, you will have belief about the size of that mustard seed. As you start receiving your goals, your belief will soar. Then as you become totally aware of your words, you will notice that your words become reality on every little detail.

While writing this book, two small things came into my life that verified what I said about being aware of my words. The first happened during Halloween. I live on a mountain and my driveway is very long and steep. All the houses on my street are far apart and each driveway is long and steep. Normally, we do not get trick-or-treaters. About five days before Halloween, I noticed my neighbor with his two young kids in their driveway across the street. My intuition told me they would come over trick-or-treating on Halloween. I suggested to my wife that she buy candy. Each day until Halloween I kept asking her to get candy. She kept forgetting. My younger daughter assured me no one would come knocking at my door on Halloween night. I kept repeating that I had a feeling someone would. Guess what? I had 20 kids come for candy on Halloween. I have never had anyone come in the eleven years since we have been in our house.

Was this a coincidence or was my self talk that powerful?

Another thing happened to me while shopping at a Staples store. I noticed one of the one cup coffee makers that everyone seems to be using. I thought about getting one. I told my wife about it. I kept thinking about getting one, but never made it a priority. A few days later I got a call from my brother. He told me he bought three of them and got one for me. We never talked about a coffee maker. He had no idea I decided on one. When I told my brother I was thinking of the coffee maker and thanked him for giving one to me, he said, "I think you are controlling my mind. Please don't think about my Corvette. I want to keep it myself for awhile and I am thinking I am going to end up giving it to you if you start thinking of it."

First, you cannot control another person's mind. You will have your hands full controlling your own thinking.
Lastly, I love my Porsche so he has nothing to worry about.

I recommend you begin heeding the above stated advice. Do not wait another minute. Do it today!

Ron Piscitelli
San Diego, California

Watch your words; they become thoughts.
Watch your thoughts; they become your self image.
Watch your self image; it becomes your destiny...

Ron Piscitelli
Chant Your Goals

About the Author

www.RonPiscitelli.com

Ron Piscitelli is available for private coaching and for speaking engagements.
For information, call: (800) 251-7805

Ron is the President of Global Building Services and has been for over 30 years.

He is the author of the book **Coffee Break Wisdom on Starting a Successful Business.**

He is also the author of **Pasta FaZool for the Soul.** A cook book featuring Italian recipes and family history.

He is the author of the book,
Jump Into Janitorial. A book on how to build a janitorial business netting over six figures a year. Visit that site at:
www.JumpIntoJanitorial.com

He is the author of 24 children's books that teach kids business savvy, called **Kids Playing Business.**
www.KidsPlayingBusiness.com

Ron is married to wife Ellen and they have been together for forty years. They have two beautiful daughters Pia and Alex and family dog Lucy.

He was born in Brockton, Massachusetts, a graduate of Bridgewater State University in Massachusetts and now lives in San Diego, California.

www.RonPiscitelli.com

Made in the USA
Charleston, SC
06 July 2012